# A WORLD OF

# PLANTS

## MARTIN JENKINS & JAMES BROWN

### CANDLEWICK STUDIO

# CONTENTS

# THE WONDERFUL WORLD OF PLANTS

**Welcome to the world of plants. They're marvelous things, I'm sure you'll agree—though you may be surprised to find out just how marvelous. But can you say exactly what a plant is?**

**THAT'S AN EASY QUESTION** to ask but not such a simple one to answer. A green thing with leaves? Usually, but not always. Something that has flowers and comes from a seed? Mostly, but there are a good 30,000 kinds of plants that don't come from seeds. Something that grows in the ground? Again, lots of plants do, but there are some that spend their whole lives perched high up on other plants and others that float in water or cling to rocks.

In fact plants are a hugely variable group. There are tiny ones and huge ones—some plants are the biggest living things on the planet by far. There are plants that live for a few weeks and others that can survive for thousands of years. There are plants that shoot out their seeds at 155 miles/250 kilometers an hour, ones that eat animals, and ones that steal all their nourishment from other plants.

One thing we can certainly say about plants is that they are smarter than we might think. They fight one another and sometimes help one another out, communicating in ways we are only just beginning to understand. They form alliances with fungi and microbes and have evolved all kinds of cunning ways to trick animals into working for them. They have also evolved lots of clever ways to avoid being eaten by animals, and some actually trap and eat animals themselves.

But perhaps the most important thing about plants is that we are utterly dependent on them. Without them, and in particular the one thing that they (almost all) do, we simply wouldn't be here at all.

# THE MOST IMPORTANT REACTION

**Plants are remarkable for all sorts of reasons. But they are probably most remarkable for the fact that they can create themselves pretty much out of water and thin air.**

**U**SING A PROCESS known as photosynthesis, most plants harness energy from sunlight to combine carbon dioxide (which is composed of carbon and oxygen) with water (composed of hydrogen and oxygen) to make large, complicated chemicals known as organic molecules. These are, literally, the stuff of life.

Like other living things, plants are formed of cells—bags of living matter called cytoplasm surrounded by a membrane, all made out of organic molecules. Photosynthesis takes place inside special bodies in the cytoplasm called chloroplasts. For chloroplasts to work, the cells that contain them need to be exposed to sunlight. This is essentially what leaves are: chloroplast-rich cells arranged to capture the maximum amount of energy from the sun. For photosynthesis to take place, carbon dioxide and water have to reach the chloroplasts. Carbon dioxide exists as a gas in the atmosphere and enters leaves through little openings called stomata. Water, which plants need

> **We are totally reliant on plants for food and energy.**

for more than just photosynthesis, is usually absorbed from the ground through roots and transported to the leaves in special channels inside the plant.

The molecules produced in the chloroplasts are carbohydrates—a combination of carbon, oxygen, and hydrogen. Other processes in cells turn these into organic molecules that are needed for life, chiefly proteins and nucleic acids (RNA and DNA). These contain additional chemical elements, most importantly sulfur, phosphorus, and nitrogen, which plants get from soil. The organic molecules produced by photosynthesis are incredibly important and are used by a host of living things.

# PHOTOSYNTHESIS

Plants harness energy from the sun to combine carbon dioxide with water. This allows them to produce carbohydrates that provide them with energy.

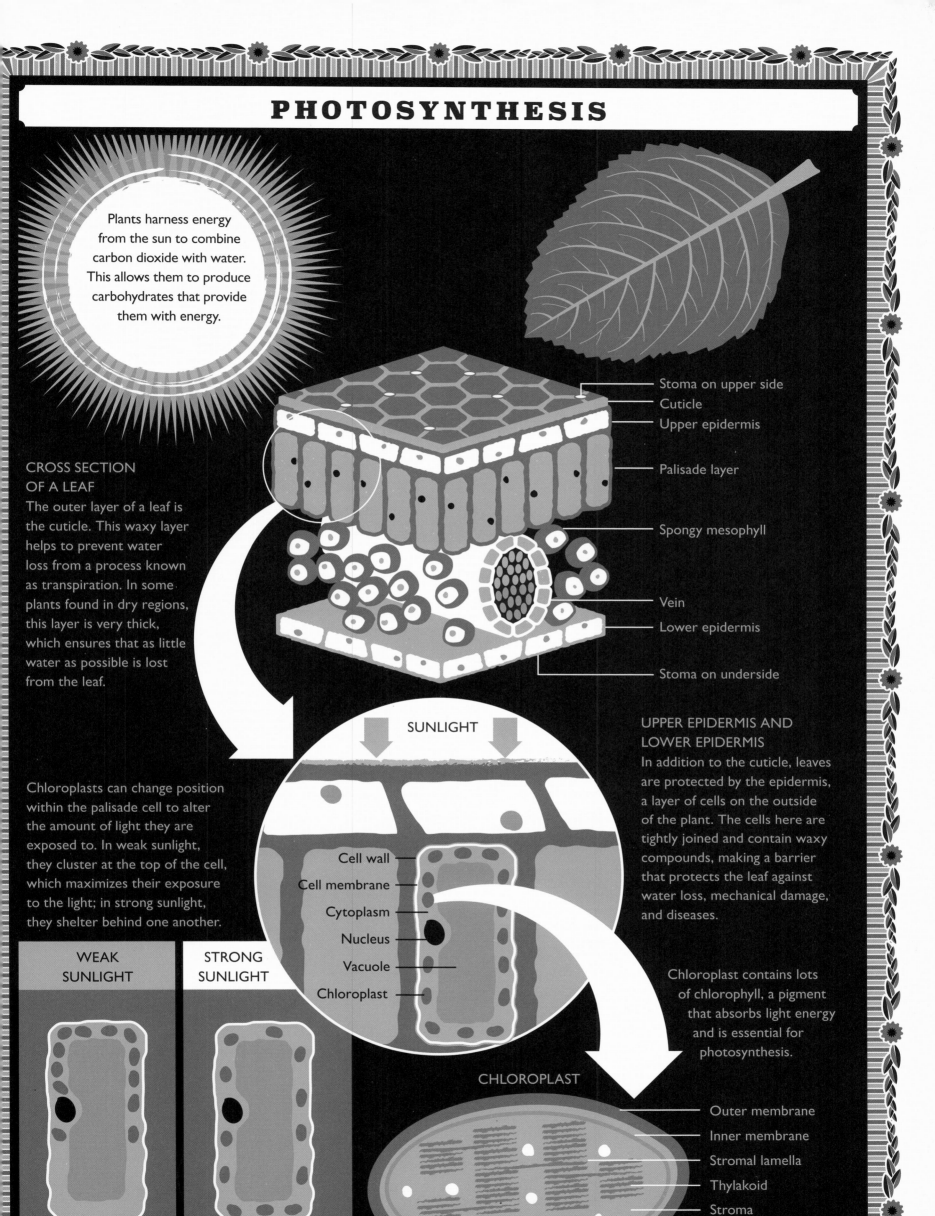

## CROSS SECTION OF A LEAF

The outer layer of a leaf is the cuticle. This waxy layer helps to prevent water loss from a process known as transpiration. In some plants found in dry regions, this layer is very thick, which ensures that as little water as possible is lost from the leaf.

Chloroplasts can change position within the palisade cell to alter the amount of light they are exposed to. In weak sunlight, they cluster at the top of the cell, which maximizes their exposure to the light; in strong sunlight, they shelter behind one another.

- Stoma on upper side
- Cuticle
- Upper epidermis
- Palisade layer
- Spongy mesophyll
- Vein
- Lower epidermis
- Stoma on underside

SUNLIGHT

- Cell wall
- Cell membrane
- Cytoplasm
- Nucleus
- Vacuole
- Chloroplast

## UPPER EPIDERMIS AND LOWER EPIDERMIS

In addition to the cuticle, leaves are protected by the epidermis, a layer of cells on the outside of the plant. The cells here are tightly joined and contain waxy compounds, making a barrier that protects the leaf against water loss, mechanical damage, and diseases.

Chloroplast contains lots of chlorophyll, a pigment that absorbs light energy and is essential for photosynthesis.

### WEAK SUNLIGHT

Chloroplasts in weak light

### STRONG SUNLIGHT

Chloroplasts in strong light

### CHLOROPLAST

- Outer membrane
- Inner membrane
- Stromal lamella
- Thylakoid
- Stroma
- Starch/Sugar

# CYCLING CARBON

**Plants don't just make the world's food through photosynthesis. They produce the oxygen we need to breathe and play a vital role in regulating the Earth's climate. That's quite an impressive list of achievements!**

**U**SING PHOTOSYNTHESIS, plants make the organic molecules that nonphotosynthesizing organisms—and that includes all animals, even humans—need as food. But there's more to it than that. All the oxygen in the atmosphere is also the result of photosynthesis. It's good that it's there because most living things, including plants themselves (and humans), depend on it to survive. It's used to release the energy that cells need from organic molecules in a process known as aerobic respiration. In addition to releasing energy, aerobic respiration produces carbon dioxide and water. It is essentially photosynthesis in reverse and is very similar to what happens when you burn wood, coal, or oil.

**Carbon moving around the Earth enables us to live and grow.**

So, plants operate on a kind of cycle, taking carbon dioxide from the atmosphere and, along with animals, fungi, and other living things, releasing it again as they respire. All this forms one vital part of the carbon cycle, the immensely complicated system by which carbon moves around different parts of the Earth, from high in the atmosphere to deep below its crust.

The carbon cycle itself plays a hugely important part in regulating Earth's climate. That's because carbon dioxide is a greenhouse gas—it traps a high proportion of the heat that reaches us from the sun in the atmosphere, which means that the more carbon dioxide there is, the warmer Earth gets. Photosynthesizing organisms do an amazingly good job at limiting the amount of carbon dioxide in the atmosphere, which in turn moderates the climate. We humans have disrupted this system by burning fossil fuels that have released vast amounts of carbon dioxide into the atmosphere in a very short space of time, causing the planet to overheat. It's essential that we reduce our carbon output to restore balance to the cycle.

8

# THE CARBON CYCLE

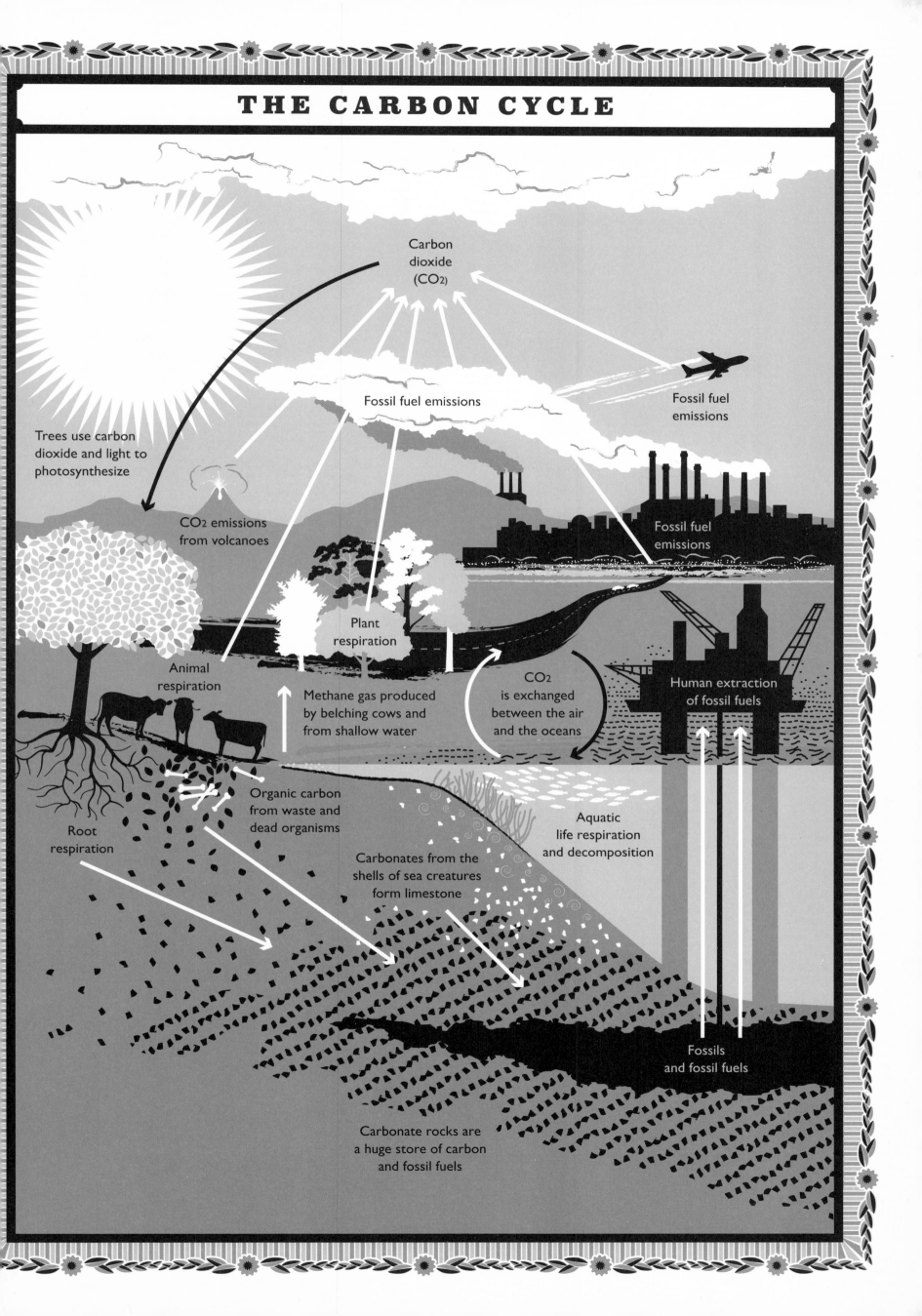

Carbon dioxide ($CO_2$)

Trees use carbon dioxide and light to photosynthesize

$CO_2$ emissions from volcanoes

Fossil fuel emissions

Fossil fuel emissions

Fossil fuel emissions

Plant respiration

Animal respiration

Methane gas produced by belching cows and from shallow water

$CO_2$ is exchanged between the air and the oceans

Human extraction of fossil fuels

Root respiration

Organic carbon from waste and dead organisms

Carbonates from the shells of sea creatures form limestone

Aquatic life respiration and decomposition

Fossils and fossil fuels

Carbonate rocks are a huge store of carbon and fossil fuels

# THE PLANT FAMILY TREE

**Modern-day plants may vary hugely, but they have one thing in common: they are all descended from a single ancestor that colonized land sometime over 450 million years ago.**

**P**LANTS ARE very good at photosynthesis, but they didn't invent it. Water-dwelling bacteria did that, more than two billion years ago. Their direct descendants, called cyanobacteria, are still the main photosynthesizers in the oceans. After bacteria came various kinds of aquatic algae. Then, probably around 475 million years ago, at least one and probably several forms of algae evolved to live on land. One was the ancestor of all later land plants.

**Today's plants evolved from water-dwelling bacteria.**

The first land plants were tiny, low-growing plants that lived in damp places; they probably looked something like modern-day moss, liverwort, or hornwort. They reproduced using spores—single cells with a toughened coating that could be blown by the wind or splashed around by the rain. At some point more than 420 million years ago, one of these early land plants gave rise to plants with specialized structures for transporting water and nutrients from one part of the plant to another. These were the first vascular plants. Quillworts, which grow in water, and a type of moss called sphagnum are directly descended from these and are probably little changed in appearance.

Later still, plants with stems, roots, and, in many cases, leaves appeared, among them the ancestors of today's ferns. At some stage, one of these gave rise to plants with a revolutionary way of reproducing: using seeds instead of spores. The original seed-bearing plants evolved into a number of different forms, including the ancestors of modern-day conifers and cycads. These took over from ferns as the dominant plants on land. Then, perhaps sometime around 140 million years ago, something else entirely new evolved from one of these: plants with flowers.

# THE PLANT FAMILY TREE

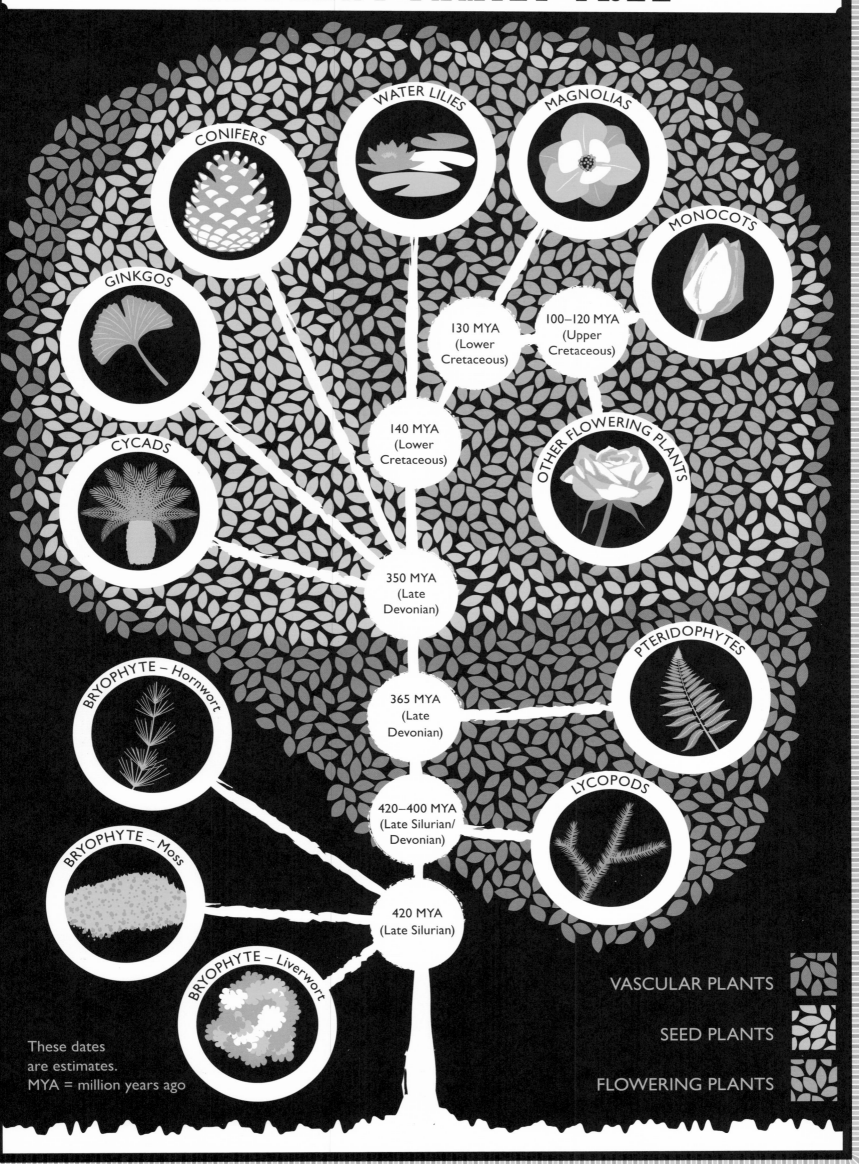

WATER LILIES

MAGNOLIAS

CONIFERS

GINKGOS

MONOCOTS

130 MYA
(Lower Cretaceous)

100–120 MYA
(Upper Cretaceous)

140 MYA
(Lower Cretaceous)

CYCADS

OTHER FLOWERING PLANTS

350 MYA
(Late Devonian)

PTERIDOPHYTES

BRYOPHYTE – Hornwort

365 MYA
(Late Devonian)

420–400 MYA
(Late Silurian/Devonian)

LYCOPODS

BRYOPHYTE – Moss

420 MYA
(Late Silurian)

BRYOPHYTE – Liverwort

VASCULAR PLANTS

SEED PLANTS

FLOWERING PLANTS

These dates
are estimates.
MYA = million years ago

# THE SECRET LIFE OF FLOWERS

**As with animals, by far the most common way that plants reproduce is through sex. Sex is when two cells, usually of very different sizes, fuse together to form a new cell.**

**I**N FLOWERING PLANTS, all this happens in the flowers themselves. The small cells, known as sperm cells, develop in pollen, which is produced in organs called anthers. The large egg cells develop in ovules in a different part of the flower called the carpel. The carpel has an elongated part, the style, that opens out into an area called the stigma.

In most flowering plants, fertilization goes something like this: A pollen grain lands on a stigma. It absorbs water and swells up, sending out a tube that goes through the stigma and down the style until it reaches an ovule, which it enters through a tiny opening. Meanwhile a cell in the pollen tube divides to form two sperm cells that don't have outer membranes. These move down the tube into the ovule. One of them fertilizes the egg cell. This fertilized egg cell is called a zygote, and it will start to grow into an embryo. The other sperm cell fuses with more cells in the ovule and forms something called an endosperm. This serves as a food store for the embryo when it starts to grow.

**A stigma is often hairy or sticky, effective for trapping pollen.**

Of course, a pollen grain has to land on a stigma for all this to happen in the first place. Many flowers have both anthers and carpels, so you might think this would be easy. However, it's generally much better if fertilization takes place between different plants of the same kind. Somehow pollen has to get from one plant to another. There are several ways this can happen, but by far the most significant is through animals, especially insects, and, above all, bees.

12

# FERTILIZATION OF FLOWERS

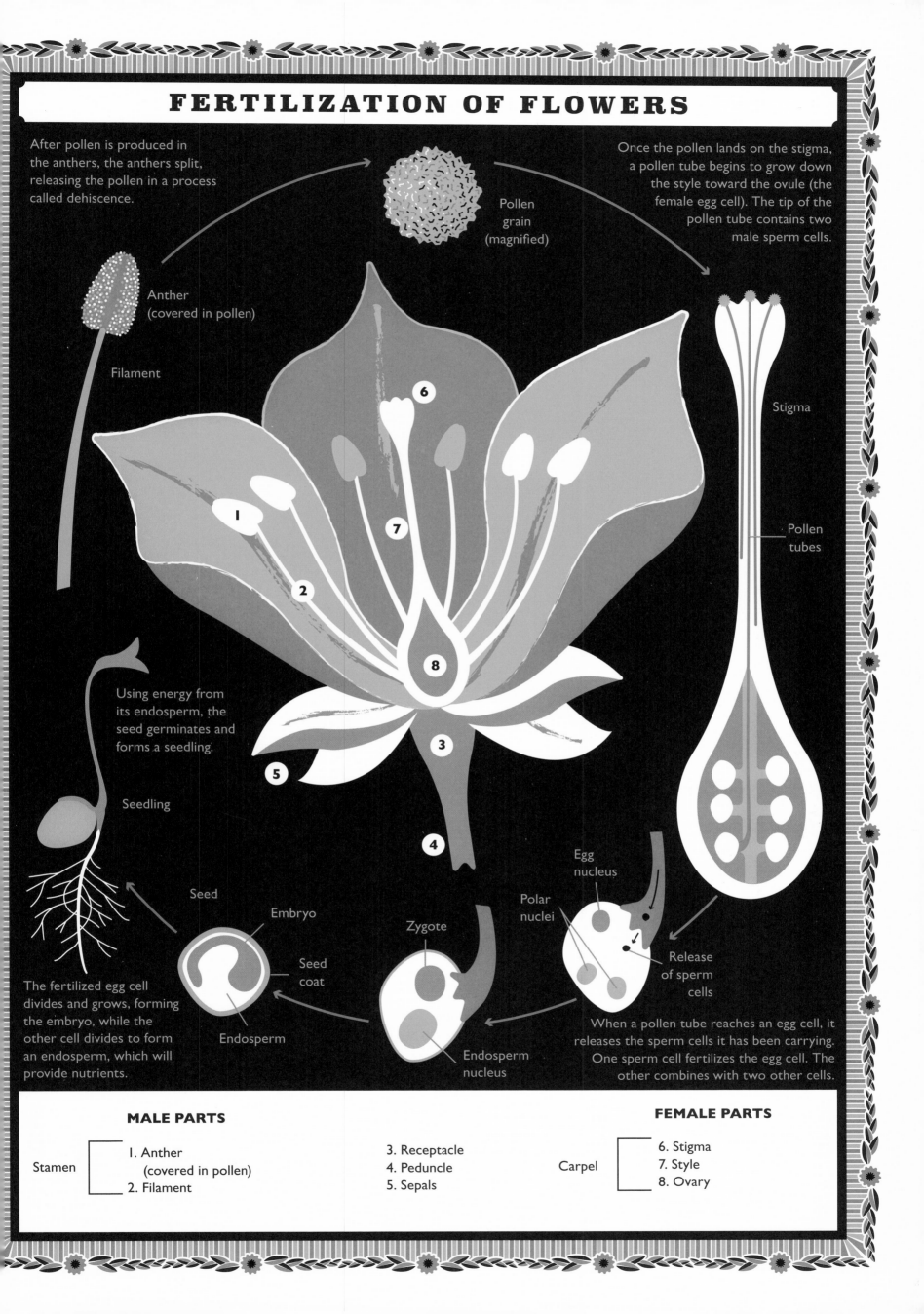

After pollen is produced in the anthers, the anthers split, releasing the pollen in a process called dehiscence.

Pollen grain (magnified)

Once the pollen lands on the stigma, a pollen tube begins to grow down the style toward the ovule (the female egg cell). The tip of the pollen tube contains two male sperm cells.

Anther (covered in pollen)

Filament

Stigma

Pollen tubes

Using energy from its endosperm, the seed germinates and forms a seedling.

Seedling

Seed

Embryo

Seed coat

Endosperm

The fertilized egg cell divides and grows, forming the embryo, while the other cell divides to form an endosperm, which will provide nutrients.

Zygote

Endosperm nucleus

Egg nucleus

Polar nuclei

Release of sperm cells

When a pollen tube reaches an egg cell, it releases the sperm cells it has been carrying. One sperm cell fertilizes the egg cell. The other combines with two other cells.

**MALE PARTS**

Stamen
- 1. Anther (covered in pollen)
- 2. Filament

3. Receptacle
4. Peduncle
5. Sepals

**FEMALE PARTS**

Carpel
- 6. Stigma
- 7. Style
- 8. Ovary

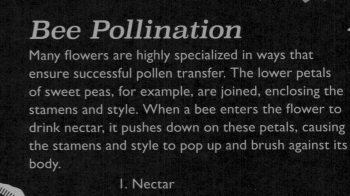

## Bee Pollination

Many flowers are highly specialized in ways that ensure successful pollen transfer. The lower petals of sweet peas, for example, are joined, enclosing the stamens and style. When a bee enters the flower to drink nectar, it pushes down on these petals, causing the stamens and style to pop up and brush against its body.

1. Nectar
2. Peduncle
3. Pollen-covered anther
4. Pollen-covered bee

**B**EES AND FLOWERS are made for each other. There are around 20,000 kinds of bees, and almost all of them depend on flowers for their food. In turn, flowering plants rely on the bees to carry pollen from one flower to another for fertilization.

It works like this: Flowers use colors and delicious scents to attract bees, which they then reward with two kinds of food: sugary nectar, and pollen, which is rich in fats and proteins. The foraging bees gather the pollen on their furry bodies and carry it back to their nest wrapped around their legs or on their underside.

Flowers normally produce nectar at the base of the carpel, so a visiting bee has to push past the flower's stigma to get at it. If the bee is already carrying pollen from another flower, with luck some of it will get brushed off onto the stigma, allowing fertilization to take place.

14

# Carrion Fly Pollination

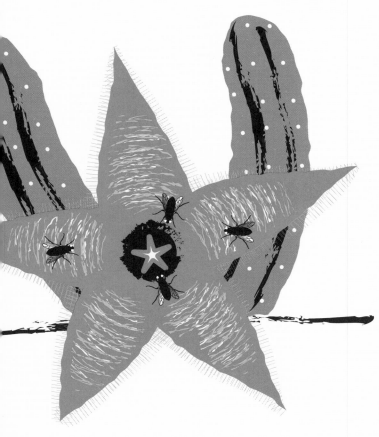

...owfly maggots feed on dead animals. Stapelia flowers look ...d smell like rotting meat and attract blowflies that lay their ...gs on them, pollinating them in the process. By the time ... fly eggs hatch, the flower has already withered away.

# Bird Pollination

Hummingbirds and sunbirds play a big role in pollinating plants in warmer parts of the world. The flowers of plants they pollinate, including various kinds of honeysuckle, are often tube-shaped, with the nectar hidden deep down at the base.

# Wind Pollination

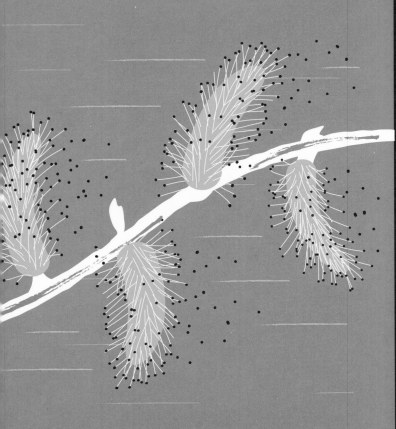

...any trees, including willows, that flower in late winter or ...rly spring, when flying insects are scarce, rely on the wind ... pollination. The male flowers have large numbers of ...thers that release copious quantities of pollen into the air.

# Bat Pollination

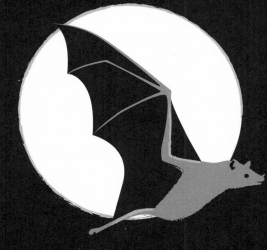

The flowers of plants pollinated by bats—including several kinds of large cacti—open at night and give off powerful scents that can attract the bats from long distances. The flowers are usually large, with broad, open faces.

# SEEDS

**Seeds are one of evolution's greatest inventions. Nine out of ten living plant species reproduce with them. Most of these are flowering plants, but not all—many familiar trees, including pines, firs, and spruces, do not flower but also produce seeds.**

IN THESE PLANTS, rather than being protected inside a carpel, the ovule grows directly on the surface of the parent plant, usually inside a cone. These plants are called gymnosperms. With most of them, pollination is by wind, but in some, especially cycads, beetles and other insects play an important part.

In both flowering plants and gymnosperms, the result of pollination is a seed: a plant in waiting, usually with some food to get it started in life and a protective coating, called an integument. The seeds of flowering plants are often further wrapped in a fruit, formed from the carpel of the parent plant.

Seeds are amazingly variable. The biggest, that of the coco-de-mer palm, can weigh over 37 pounds/17 kilograms, while some orchid seeds weigh less than a millionth of a gram. All of them

**Coco-de-mer palms are only found in the Seychelles and their seeds are highly prized.**

have the purpose of turning into adult plants. The beginning of this process is called germination. Usually this starts when a root appears, which anchors the seed in place and starts to draw water in. Then a shoot develops, generally sporting one or more leaves, ready to start the important business of photosynthesis. The first leaves are known as cotyledons and are usually different from any the plant will later produce.

For a seed to successfully grow into an adult plant, it needs to start off in the right place—somewhere where the amount of light and moisture and whatever it's growing in (soil, usually) suit it. The spot where the parent plant is growing is an obvious place, but of course that is generally occupied. Plants therefore need a way to spread their seeds around. They have evolved many ingenious ways of doing so, many of which, as with pollination, involve animals.

# THREE TYPES OF SEEDS

## Sunflower

DICOT SEED

Sunflower seeds need light to germinate.

Like the seeds of all dicots, the sunflower seed produces two tiny seed leaves.

The case of the seed contains chemicals that prevent other plants from growing, ensuring that the sunflower gets enough space and nutrients.

## Sweet pea

DICOT SEED

Sweet pea seeds develop in pods.

The pods explode, throwing the seeds away from their parent plant.

Its two seed leaves stay under the soil, where they are protected from marauding insects.

## Lily

The lily germinates to produce one seed leaf.

There are two main types of lily seed germination: immediate and delayed.

Seeds with delayed germination require both a warm and a cold period.

MONOCOT SEED

## Corn

A corn kernel is actually the seed coat and the ovary joined tightly together.

Corn is a monocot and produces a single seed leaf.

Instead of getting energy from within this leaf, the growing seedling gets energy from the endosperm of the seed.

MONOCOT SEED

## Conifer

GYMNOSPERM SEED

Conifer seeds are gymnosperms, which means "naked seeds" and indicates that their unfertilized seeds have no protective covering.

Conifer seeds are found on cones.

Each conifer tree produces many seeds, but only a few will germinate.

## Cycad

GYMNOSPERM SEED

Cycads also have seeds that are uncovered.

Cycad seeds can take up to nine months to ripen before they can germinate.

Their seed leaves are small and easily missed, but the seeds are large, weighing as much as an ounce/25 grams.

Many plants' seeds are encased in tasty fruit, encouraging birds and other animals to eat them. The seeds themselves pass through the animals' guts intact and are ready to grow whenever and wherever they are finally deposited.

Squirrels, like many other rodents, eat acorns and othe[r] seeds, using their sharp teeth to gnaw through their prote[ctive] coating. They often also bury them as a reserve for times [of] shortage. They rarely dig up all the seeds they bury, leavin[g] others to sprout when conditions are right.

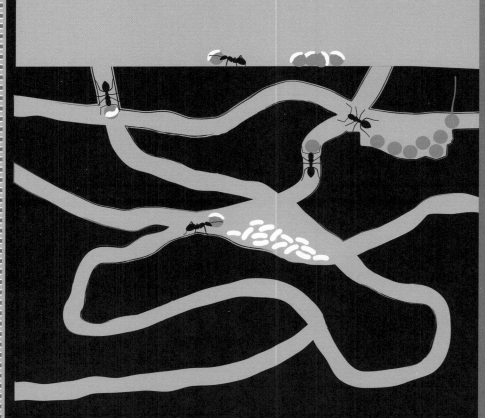

Instead of making fruits, some plants produce seeds that have a tasty, nutritious outgrowth attached, called an aril. These are particularly attractive to ants. They carry the seeds off to their nests, where they eat the arils and discard the seeds, which may then sprout.

Some plants produce seedpods that are covered in hooks or bristles. These get caught in the fur or feathers (or socks) of passing animals and are carried along until they are rubbed or picked off.

...e seeds are carried away by water. Coconuts are buoyant ...d can travel vast distances on ocean currents, sometimes germinating while they are still afloat.

The sandbox tree has explosive fruits. As they dry out, the casing of each seed squeezes together until the seed is suddenly ejected with a loud crack at a speed of up to 155 miles/250 kilometers per hour. This is called ballistic seed dispersal.

...andelions and thistles, individual seeds break off from the ...wer head. They are usually very light, with parachute-like attachments that catch the wind.

Plants that grow in grasslands and other open places often rely on the wind to carry their seeds. Sometimes the whole flower head dries out and forms a ball that detaches from the parent plant and rolls along, scattering seeds as it goes.

# SPORES

**The first land plants reproduced using spores instead of seeds. A range of plants still does so, mostly dwellers of damp places, such as mosses, liverworts, and ferns.**

**A**LTHOUGH IN THE modern world there are far fewer kinds of spore-producing than seed-producing plants, spore producers can't be written off as unimportant or primitive. Among them are some very successful plants that play vital roles in ecosystems all around the world, from Arctic tundra to tropical cloud forest.

Spore-producing plants still reproduce using sex, but they do so in a very different way from flowering plants. In ferns there are two quite distinct generations. The plant that we think of as the actual fern is the one that produces spores and is known as the sporophyte generation. The spores themselves are single cells with a tough coating that are blown around by the wind.

If the spore lands where conditions are right, it will start to grow by cell division. Eventually it forms a small plantlet called a prothallus that looks nothing like the parent sporophyte. This is the gametophyte generation. Two different kinds of reproductive organs develop on the prothallus: ones that produce sperm and ones that produce eggs. In some ferns one prothallus may have both kinds and in others each individual prothallus has one or the other, but not both.

As in seed plants (and animals), reproduction takes place when a sperm fertilizes an egg cell. Ferns and other spore-bearing plants have no pollen grains to carry the sperm cells around, so the sperm has to reach the egg cell by itself. It does this by swimming. For this reason, these plants can reproduce sexually only where and when it is damp enough for a film of water to form on the surface of the prothallus.

For fertilization to take place in ferns, a sperm usually has to make the journey from one prothallus to another. Fortunately, adult ferns usually produce huge numbers of spores, and when conditions are right, many end up growing crowded together, forming a continuous surface for the sperm to swim over.

**The little brown bumps on the underside of a fern leaf contain its spores.**

20

# THE LIFE OF A FERN

The furry structures you can sometimes see on the underside of fern leaves are clusters of sporangia: the structures that produce and hold spores.

Spores

Sporangium

Sorus

When the spores are ready, the outside of the sporangium breaks open and releases them. If the conditions are right, the cells in the spore divide and it grows into a small heart-shaped structure called a gametophyte.

Young gametophyte

Underside of leaf

Mature male gametophyte

Mature female gametophyte

Mature sporophyte

Sperm

Egg

Fiddlehead

New sporophyte

Gametophyte

The zygote then grows by cell division to produce a new fern plant. New fern fronds are curled up and look a bit like the end of a violin, so they are called fiddleheads.

Zygote

Sperm is produced by a mature male gametophyte and eggs by a mature female gametophyte. The sperm has a tail, which it uses to swim through water to reach an egg. It then fertilizes the egg, forming a zygote.

# HOW PLANTS SPREAD

Besides reproducing by sex, many plants have other, often very successful, ways of increasing in number—it's yet another example of how much they differ from animals.

## Division

Floating water plants such as duckweed and common water hyacinth grow by division, budding off new plantlets in rapid succession. Some kinds of duckweed can double in number in fewer than two days.

## Bulbs, Corms, and Tube[rs]

Many plants produce storage organs from [s] leaf bases, stems, or roots, which they use [t] through periods when conditions aren't rig[ht for] growth. Each plant may produce many of th[ese] organs as it goes into dormancy, each of wh[ich] can in turn grow as a separate plant the foll[owing] season. Usually these organs form undergr[ound,] but in some cases, as with lilies and snowdr[ops,] for example, they may form along the stem[.]

## Stolons and Rhizomes

Plants such as strawberries send out special stems known as runners or stolons, which have plantlets growing along them; each plantlet can take root where it meets the ground.

## Stem Rooting

Brambles have long arching stems that normally scramble through other plants but can also take root where they meet the ground.

## ...ves and Stem Pads

...cculent plants that live in dry places have ...oosely attached leaves, which are easily ... by passing animals or in the wind or heavy ...tached leaf can put out roots and grow ...w plant. Some cacti, such as prickly pears, ... pads that behave in the same way.

## Plantlets on Leaves

The Madagascan succulent kalanchoe makes tiny plantlets along the edges of its leaves, each with leaves and roots. These may be dislodged by rain or animals and can quickly take root in damp soil.

## Root Suckers

Many trees and shrubs— including laurel, aralia, and coyote willow—have spreading roots that sprout new stems some distance from the parent plant, especially if the root itself is damaged.

...ants, including lily of the valley ...oo, have stems called rhizomes, ...w along or under the ground ...ut roots and new shoots as they

# THE FIGHT FOR LIGHT

**Light is a precious resource for plants—without it, they cannot make their food. Access to light is something they compete with one another for, and trees do so remarkably effectively.**

**T**HE OBVIOUS way for a plant to get ahead is to overgrow its neighbors, reaching up and spreading out to intercept the sunlight before it reaches the others. However, to do this, a plant needs either something to climb or the ability to support itself. It also needs ways to carry water and mineral nutrients from the soil up into its aerial parts, and the products of photosynthesis from these parts to the rest of it.

Vascular plants do this with the help of two different kinds of tissue that run through the plant: xylem carries water and mineral nutrients, and phloem carries the products of photosynthesis. Both xylem and phloem contain specialized cells that do the actual transporting, arranged as bundles of tubes. In phloem, these cells are still alive and have relatively thin cell walls, while in xylem they are dead and usually have thick, toughened cell walls, containing a high proportion of a very strong material called lignin. When a lot of xylem cells are bundled together, they create stiff rods that can hold the plant stem containing them upright.

> **Trees are the longest-living organisms on the planet.**

In some plants, new xylem and phloem cells form only at the growing tip of the stem, so the stem does not thicken much as it grows, which puts a limit on how strong it can get. In others, a tissue called cambium sits between the xylem and phloem and produces new cells of each, allowing the stem to grow thicker and stronger. In some of these plants, the xylem and phloem cells are arranged in bundles scattered through the stem, but in others the xylem forms a solid core at the middle, with the cambium in a ring around it. As the cambium produces more xylem, the older xylem, toward the middle of the core, stops being used for transporting water and becomes compressed and hard. The new and old xylem combined form wood, the stuff that holds trees up—and one of the most important and remarkable substances in nature.

24

# HOW TREES WORK

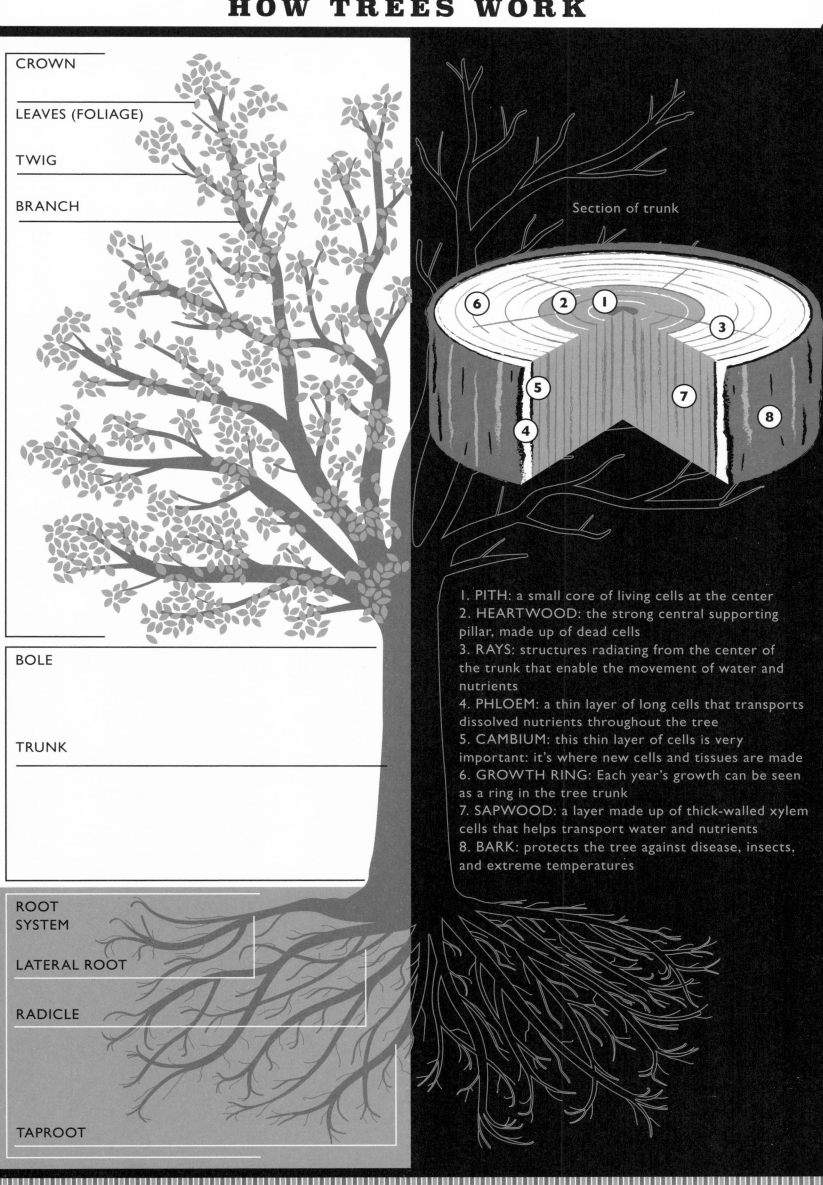

CROWN

LEAVES (FOLIAGE)

TWIG

BRANCH

BOLE

TRUNK

ROOT SYSTEM

LATERAL ROOT

RADICLE

TAPROOT

Section of trunk

1. PITH: a small core of living cells at the center
2. HEARTWOOD: the strong central supporting pillar, made up of dead cells
3. RAYS: structures radiating from the center of the trunk that enable the movement of water and nutrients
4. PHLOEM: a thin layer of long cells that transports dissolved nutrients throughout the tree
5. CAMBIUM: this thin layer of cells is very important: it's where new cells and tissues are made
6. GROWTH RING: Each year's growth can be seen as a ring in the tree trunk
7. SAPWOOD: a layer made up of thick-walled xylem cells that helps transport water and nutrients
8. BARK: protects the tree against disease, insects, and extreme temperatures

# TALL, TALLER, TALLEST TREES

Plants don't need wood to grow tall, but it helps. Tree ferns, cycads, and bamboos all have various kinds of toughened fiber that strengthens and supports their stems, enabling them to reach impressive heights. Able to grow a bit taller are the ginkgo—the sole survivor of an ancient lineage related to cycads, which has conifer-like wood—and palms, which, like bamboo, are monocotyledons and have an unusual wood-like tissue quite different from that of other trees. But these are overshadowed by numerous wood-bearing plants, of which the very tallest are various kinds of conifer and dicotyledons. Curiously, although there are some very tall trees in the tropics, the tallest trees are found in temperate (mild) parts of the world. Botanists are still trying to figure out why.

**1. Hope's cycad (*Lepidozamia hopei*)** Found in Australia, with specimens reaching 66 feet/20 meters tall, this is thought to be the tallest cycad species in the world.

**2. Norfolk tree fern (*Cyathea brownii*)** Found on Norfolk Island in the Pacific Ocean, this is thought to be the tallest fern, growing to more than 66 feet/20 meters.

**3. Giant bamboo or dragon bamboo (*Dendrocalamus giganteus*)** Found in Southeast Asia, this is the tallest species of grass. It grows very fast (up to 16 inches/40 centimeters a day) and typically reaches around 98 feet/30 meters in height, with specimens reaching 138 feet/42 meters.

**4. Ginkgo or maidenhair tree (*Ginkgo biloba*)** The only surviving species of its group; some ginkgos growing in China have reached 164 feet/50 meters tall.

**5. Palma de cera (*Ceroxylon quindiuense*)** Found in the Andes, this is the tallest palm tree, reaching heights of 197 feet/60 meters.

**6. Yellow meranti (*Shorea faguetiana*)** The tallest tropical tree is a 300-foot-/93-meter-tall yellow meranti growing in Borneo.

**7. Mountain ash (*Eucalyptus regnans*)** The mountain ash is not only the tallest dicot but also the tallest flowering plant in the world. The largest specimen is in Tasmania and is 327 feet/99.8 meters tall.

**8. Coast redwood (*Sequoia sempervirens*)** The tallest tree in the world is a conifer. These are also some of the oldest living things (more than 1,000 years old) and can grow up to 380 feet/115.5 meters in height.

377 ft./115 m
361 ft./110 m
344 ft./105 m
328 ft./100 m
312 ft./95 m
295 ft./90 m
279 ft./85 m
262 ft./80 m
246 ft./75 m
230 ft./70 m
213 ft./65 m
197 ft./60 m
180 ft./55 m
164 ft./50 m
148 ft./45 m
131 ft./40 m
115 ft./35 m
98 ft./30 m
82 ft./25 m
66 ft./20 m
49 ft/15 m
33 ft./10 m
16 ft./5 m

1  2  3  4

394 ft./
120 m

377 ft./
115 m

361 ft./
110 m

344 ft./
105 m

328 ft./
100 m

312 ft./
95 m

295 ft./
90 m

279 ft./
85 m

262 ft./
80 m

246 ft./
75 m

230 ft./
70 m

213 ft./
65 m

197 ft./
60 m

180 ft./
55 m

164 ft./
50 m

148 ft./
45 m

131 ft./
40 m

115 ft./
35 m

98 ft./
30 m

82 ft./
25 m

66 ft./
20 m

49 ft/
15 m

33 ft./
10 m

16 ft./
5 m

5

6

7

8

# CLIMBING PLANTS

**The great evolutionary biologist Charles Darwin was fascinated by climbing plants and wrote the first detailed scientific study of them. He marveled at their variety and wondered why so many plants had evolved to climb.**

**T**HE ANSWER he came up with is essentially the one that holds today: climbers are basically freeloaders, adapted to steal precious sunlight from their more robust hosts. By using other plants as supports, climbers do not have to invest in strong woody stems to rise above their neighbors and can put more of the products of photosynthesis into producing flowers and fruit. There are probably other advantages, too. Raising flowering parts off the ground can make them more easily accessible to flying pollinators and help with the dispersal of seeds. It also puts tender young shoots and leaves farther out of reach of ground-dwelling herbivores.

Some plants are opportunistic climbers, often found growing along the ground. Usually these are sprawlers, with thin, many-branched stems that weave upward when they encounter a suitable support, such as a low shrub or robust perennial. Other plants have a range of more specialized adaptations for climbing, developed from different parts of the plant; stems, leaves, roots, and even flower stalks are all variously pressed into service.

**Some climbing plants use hooks to haul themselves up.**

Most climbing plants have adapted to climb up other plants, by far the most common supports in nature. Some, such as ivies and Virginia creepers, which are adept at clinging to hard surfaces, may also be found growing on cliffs and rocky outcrops. These climbers have benefited hugely from the human propensity to build things with walls and thrive in artificial environments.

Apart from the sprawlers, climbers use four main adaptations: twining stems, tendrils, clinging roots or suckers, and hooks.

# SPRAWLERS, CLINGERS, AND TWINERS

## Twiners

Twining stems are very effective for climbing up thin supports. They are less able to cope with thicker supports like tree trunks, as they tend to slip down. Examples include climbing beans and bindweed.

## Tendrils and Leaf Twiners

Tendrils can be specially modified stems, leaves, or flower stalks. In leaf twiners like clematises, the leaf stalk curls around a support but the photosynthesizing leaf remains in place. Grapevines and squash are tendril climbers.

## Clingers

Clingers have specially adapted tendrils or stem-roots that produce a sticky substance that clings to the support. Some clingers such as ivy can grow their way up almost anything.

## Hook Climbers

Climbing palms, or rattans, send long fishing rod–like structures, actually modified leaves or flower stalks, high up into the forest canopy. These have strong hooks that catch hold of vegetation and enable the palm to grow upward.

# THE CHEMICAL PLANT

**Even the simplest plant is a complicated thing. It has different parts designed to do particular jobs. These parts have to know exactly what to do and when to do it. How does a plant manage all this?**

**L**IKE ANIMALS, plants need to know where they are and what is going on around them. Roots need to grow downward into soil, stems to grow up or twist around things, leaves to turn toward the light, and flowers to form and open when they have a chance of being pollinated. All this means that plants have to be able to interact with the world around them. But they lack eyes and ears and have no nervous systems for carrying information from one part to another, nor do they have muscles or a skeleton for movement. So how do plants detect and react to the world?

It's a question that has long intrigued scientists. Much of it still remains a mystery but one thing is clear: chemicals are at the heart of it all. Plant cells produce a whole range of chemicals, known as plant hormones, which affect the way individual cells and whole parts of the plant behave.

**Plants communicate with one another in many different ways.**

Probably the most important of these, and the first ones to be discovered, are auxins. These are produced mainly in the growing tips of shoots. Like other plant hormones, they are transported around the plant in the phloem and also move from cell to cell through one-way channels in cell membranes. They play a major role in controlling all sorts of things in plants, including which parts grow and which don't, when growing tips start turning into flowers, and whether particular parts of a plant grow up or down.

Not only do auxins have a whole range of effects, but they can also operate differently in different parts of a plant. In roots, for example, a high concentration of auxins stops cells from elongating, while in stems it does just the opposite. No wonder scientists have such a tough time figuring out how the whole system fits together.

30

# PLANT HORMONES

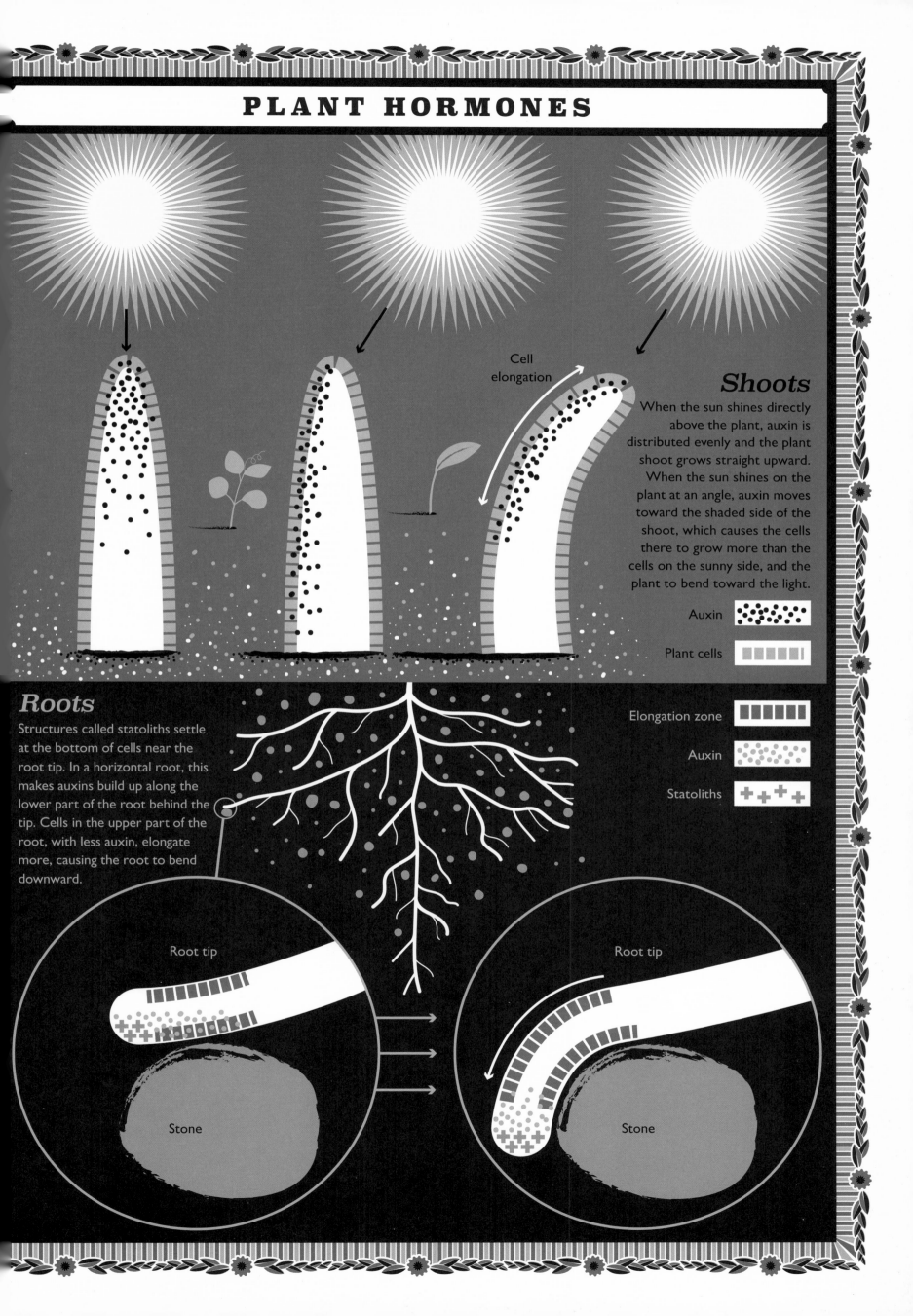

Cell elongation

## Shoots

When the sun shines directly above the plant, auxin is distributed evenly and the plant shoot grows straight upward. When the sun shines on the plant at an angle, auxin moves toward the shaded side of the shoot, which causes the cells there to grow more than the cells on the sunny side, and the plant to bend toward the light.

Auxin

Plant cells

## Roots

Structures called statoliths settle at the bottom of cells near the root tip. In a horizontal root, this makes auxins build up along the lower part of the root behind the tip. Cells in the upper part of the root, with less auxin, elongate more, causing the root to bend downward.

Elongation zone

Auxin

Statoliths

Root tip

Stone

Root tip

Stone

# WOOD-WIDE WEB

**In nature, plants never grow entirely alone. Each one is part of a complex system in which it interacts with a host of other living things: plants of its own and different species, animals, fungi, algae, and all sorts of microbes.**

**O**FTEN THESE interactions are distinctly hostile: other plants may be competing with a particular plant for resources such as sunlight and water, animals may be trying to eat it, and fungi and microbes may be stealing its nutrients and weakening or killing it in the process. But most plants also enter into cooperative arrangements with other living things—something known as mutualism or symbiosis. One of the most important of these is the way that some plants get hold of nitrogen, an element that all living things need.

Nitrogen is by far the most common substance in the atmosphere, but it's in a form that most living things can't use—nitrogen molecules. Fortunately there are microbes that can convert molecular nitrogen into a compound, ammonia, that plants can use. Some of these microbes live independently in the soil, but many can survive only in close association with plants. The plant provides the microbe with a safe environment, oxygen, and food, while the microbes furnish the plant with the ammonia it needs.

However, plants' most widespread symbiotic association is with fungi, whose threadlike bodies, called hyphae, can penetrate plants' root systems and often the actual cells in the roots. The fungus then lives in both the plant's roots and the soil. This combination of roots and fungus is called mycorrhiza. The fungus plays an important role in taking up water and mineral nutrients from the soil, some of which it passes on to the plant. In turn the plant feeds the fungus with the products of photosynthesis. What's more, hyphae from the same individual fungus can form mycorrhizas with more than one plant, effectively linking the plants' root systems. It's now known that individual plants can communicate with one another via this mycorrhizal network and are even understood to pass food to one another through it.

**Up to ninety percent of plants depend on mycorrhizas to survive.**

# PLANT INTERACTIONS

Not all interactions between plants and fungi are mutualistic. Some fungi infect plants, stealing nutrients and even sometimes directly harming the plant by producing enzymes that attack the plant's cells.

Plant roots often grow in association with fungi that have penetrated them. Since each fungus can be connected to several different plants, it is thought that the fungi's mycorrhizal networks connect the plants and carry chemical signals among them.

Some plants (mainly legumes, such as peas) have nitrogen-fixing bacteria living in nodules on their roots. These bacteria are able to absorb nitrogen from the air and convert it into a substance that the plants can use to make proteins.

# PLANTS THAT EAT ANIMALS

**In places where the mineral nutrients that plants need are in short supply, some have evolved a novel way of getting hold of them: by trapping, killing, and digesting animals.**

**I**N CERTAIN PLACES, the nutrients nitrogen and phosphorus are in particularly short supply. Ingeniously, rather than wait for things to die and decompose around them, some plants kill animals and extract what they need from their remains.

There are more than 600 species of plant that do this. Between them they have evolved a wide range of ways of catching animals. The most sophisticated are the active traps of bladderworts and venus flytraps. Bladderwort traps consist of tiny hollow swellings on stems, each of which has a trapdoor surrounded by trigger hairs. The plant pumps water out of the swelling, creating suction inside. When an animal such as a water flea presses on one of the hairs, the door springs open, sucking in water and the flea with it. The door then snaps shut with the flea trapped inside, all in less than four-thousandths of a second.

**The biggest carnivorous plants have pitchers the size of footballs.**

Other carnivorous plants are less active but still very effective. The various kinds of pitcher plants create alluring traps by mimicking flowers, producing nectar that draws in pollinating insects. Their pitchers are lined with waxy flakes that insects find hard to get a grip on. They exhaust themselves while struggling to escape and eventually drown in pools of liquid in the base of the pitchers. In some species, this liquid is a toxic acid mixture that quickly dissolves the prey, releasing chemicals that can be absorbed by the plant. In others, the liquid is much more watery and may contain bacteria and even insect larvae that feed on the drowned animals, with the plant benefiting from the waste products the bacteria and larvae produce.

34

# HOW PLANTS CATCH ANIMALS

## Flypaper

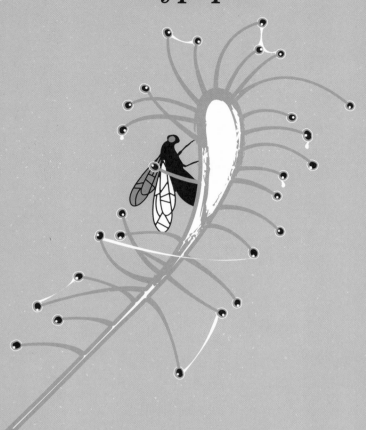

Sundew leaves are covered in tentacles that exude a sweet-scented sticky substance that attracts insects. Once one is caught, the tentacles curl inward, carrying it toward the middle of the leaf, where other glands produce digestive juices.

## Pitfall Traps

Pitcher plants come in a range of shapes and sizes. Species from temperate regions usually grow on the ground or in shallow water. In the tropics, many species are climbers or epiphytes, growing on trees in open forest.

## Snap Traps

If the trigger hairs on a Venus flytrap leaf are touched twice in quick succession, the leaf snaps shut. The struggles of a trapped insect then cause the leaf to press its edges tightly together and release juices to start digesting its prey.

## Bladderworts

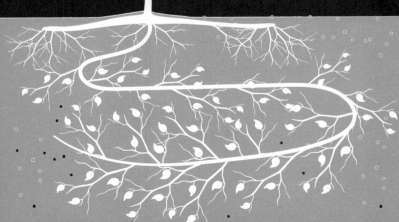

Some bladderworts are aquatic and live in freshwater ponds or streams. Their bladder traps may be as big as a thumbnail. Most species live in damp soil, often in marshes, and have tiny traps, just a few millimeters long or less.

# PLANTS THAT STEAL

**Photosynthesis is a basic feature of plants, but some species have mostly, or even entirely, given up on it. They've become parasites, relying on other plants to make their food for them.**

**A**LMOST ALL PLANTS make food themselves from carbon dioxide and water through photosynthesis. However, the freeloaders who have evolved to steal food from other plants have their own particular systems.

Instead of or in addition to normal roots, such plants have special organs called haustoria that latch on to the stems or roots of other plants and bore through to their host's vascular system, diverting the contents for their own use. The most extreme of these parasites have no chloroplasts, do not photosynthesize, and are completely dependent on their hosts. Among them are some remarkable plants such as *Rafflesia*, the world's largest flower. Other parasitic plants still do some photosynthesizing. Some of these, such as mistletoe, cannot survive without a host, while some can in theory grow independently, although even these probably rarely do so in nature and if they do, do not flourish.

> **The scientific name for some mistletoe means "thief of a tree" in Greek.**

A third group of plants still rely on other plants but do so indirectly, by parasitizing mycorrhizal fungi, which themselves get their food from photosynthesizing plants. A few of these plants may never see the light of day, even flowering just below the soil surface or under leaf litter, where they probably rely on small burrowing flies or termites for pollination.

Parasitic plants have developed ingenious ways of finding suitable hosts. Seedlings of the climbing parasite dodder can smell a host plant, and turn their stems toward it. They have to be quick, though, because they do not photosynthesize and the food reserves in their seed endosperm sustain only a few days' growth. Seeds of other species may stay dormant in the soil for years and germinate only when they detect that a host plant root has grown nearby, within a few millimeters.

# PARASITIC PLANTS

Some parasitic plants, known as hemiparasites, still carry out some photosynthesis themselves. The most familiar is probably mistletoe, which grows on trees. Since mistletoe can't survive by itself, it is called an obligate parasite. The Western Australian Christmas tree parasitizes other trees by attaching to the roots.

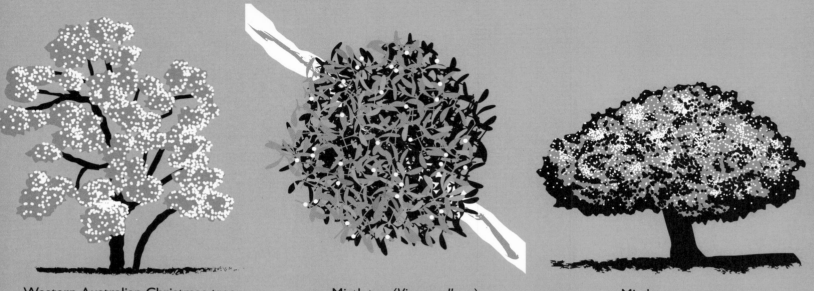

Western Australian Christmas tree

Mistletoe (*Viscum album*)

Mistletoe on a tree

Some parasitic plants do not carry out any photosynthesis themselves and would not survive without their host. Probably the most famous of these is *Rafflesia*, which grows on *Tetrastigma* vines. One of the weirdest examples is *Hydnora africana*, which grows underground (apart from a fleshy flower), taking nutrients from its host plant through the plants' roots.

Dodder (*Cuscuta europaea*)

*Rafflesia*

*Hydnora africana*

Some plants get energy and nutrients by parasitizing fungi. The snow plant is completely unable to photosynthesize and instead gets its nutrients from fungi attached to the roots of trees. It is noticeable by its red flower that pokes out from the ground. The western underground orchid remains underground. The ghost plant gains all of its nutrients from mycorrhizal fungi.

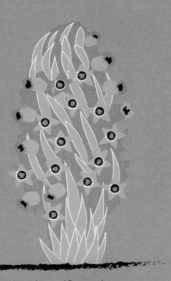

Snow plant (*Sarcodes sanguinea*)

Western underground orchid

Ghost plant (*Monotropa uniflora*)

# PLANT DEFENSES

While there are some plants that eat animals, animals that eat plants are much more common. Wherever plants grow there will be some eager to make a meal out of them. Plants have in turn come up with all sorts of responses. Plant self-defense has undoubtedly been one o major driving forces in evolution.

## Spikes on the Inside

Plants such as the dumb cane *Dieffenbachia* accumulate needlelike c of calcium minerals called raphides in their tissues while also buildi poisons. The crystals can perforate the soft lining of an animal's mc throat, allowing the poison to enter the bloodstream.

## Spikes on the Outside

Many plants protect themselves with thorns, barbs, or stinging hairs. Thorns often have unusually large numbers of microbes living on them. These can cause nasty infections in animals that get scratched.

## Mimicry

Some passionflowers and other plants develop dots on their leaves that look like butterfly eggs. Female butterflies looking for somewhere to lay their own eggs— which will hatch into caterpillars that feast on the plant—pass these leaves by.

## Hosting Defenders

...tral American bullhorn acacias like *Vachellia* ...*igera* have swollen thorns in which stinging ...ia ants (*Pseudomyrmex ferruginea*) take up ...dence. The ants fiercely defend the trees ...nst any approaching herbivores and even ...r away clinging vines and seedlings that ...ut around the tree's base. In return, ...rees feed the ants with globules of ...food produced on the edges of ...leaves and sugary nectar from ...ds on the leaf stalks.

## Calling for Help

A whole range of plants, including tobacco, corn, and cotton, release chemicals into the air when they are attacked by insects such as aphids or moths. The chemicals attract other insects that feed on the attackers. Some chemicals are very fine-tuned, attracting predators that prey on the precise insect attacking the plant.

## Tolerating Being Eaten

Grasses are adapted to being grazed on. Their growing points are close to the ground, so are unlikely to be bitten off by a grazer, and their leaves do not make an easy meal, being difficult to digest and containing gritty particles called phytoliths, which wear down the teeth or biting jaws of herbivores. Grasses are not particularly protected in other ways, though, such as through poisons or thorns. For grasses it is an advantage having some large herbivores around, because they trample on or eat seedlings of bushes or other plants that might otherwise crowd the grasses out. The animals' dung acts as an important fertilizer, too.

# THE LIVES OF PLANTS

**The life spans of plants vary as much as their appearance. Some germinate, grow, flower, set seed, and die in a matter of weeks, while others can live for thousands of years.**

WE KNOW THERE ARE PLANTS that can live for thousands of years because there are trees this old whose age can be measured with remarkable accuracy. Some trees grow in places with a seasonal climate where there is a single growing season and a single resting season each year. These trees have distinctive growth rings, one for each year. It's a relatively simple matter to take a core of wood from the living tree and count the rings. The oldest trees that have been dated in this way are bristlecone pines from the western United States, several of which have been around for nearly 5,000 years.

Unfortunately other plants don't produce such convenient records and are generally much harder to age. It's thought that tropical trees, for instance, rarely live for more than a few hundred years, although there is a sacred fig tree (the Bodhi tree) growing in a temple compound in Sri Lanka whose history can reputedly be traced back to 236 BCE. It is said to have been planted as a twig brought from India by a Buddhist nun.

There are other plants that can be considered even older. These are ones that spread underground,

**Bristlecone pines grow so slowly that their needles can remain green for forty years.**

forming colonies of aboveground parts all growing from a single huge root system. Just as plants themselves have very variable life spans, so too do their seeds or spores. Some are very short lived, and die if they do not germinate within a few weeks of ripening. Others can show extraordinary longevity: 2,000-year-old seeds of date palms and 1,300-year-old sacred lotus seeds have been successfully germinated. The record holder, however, is the campion, or catchfly, from Siberia . . .

40

## Siberian Catchfly

In 2007, scientists discovered some 32,0000-year-old unripe fruit of a catchfly, or campion, in ancient squirrel burrows deep in the Siberian permafrost. They raised plants from these fruit, which went on to flower and produce healthy seedlings.

## Bristlecone Pine

Methuselah, a bristlecone pine growing in California, is the oldest confirmed living tree (there may be one a few years older). It is believed to have sprouted in 2833 BCE, 250 years before the great pyramid of Cheops was built.

## Quick Plants

Some plants can complete their life cycle in a very short time. One of the quickest is mouse-ear cress (*Arabidopsis thaliana*), which can germinate, grow, flower, set seed, and die in just six weeks. Not surprisingly, it's a very popular plant for scientists to study in labs.

## Trembling Aspen

Trembling aspens spread through suckering roots as well as by seed. Each colony grown by suckering is basically a single organism, which can reach an enormous size and a great age. The largest and probably oldest known is called Pando, which grows in Utah, covers about 100 acres/40 hectares, and is thought to be at least 80,000 years old. No single part of it is that ancient, however—the individual tree trunks are mostly just a century or two old.

# WHAT'S IN THE GROUND

**You may not have given much thought to soil, but this seemingly unexciting mixture of rocky material, dissolved minerals, and organic matter is essential for the growth of many plants.**

SOIL NOT ONLY HOLDS the nutrients and water that plants depend on; it also anchors the roots, allowing plants to stand up above the ground.

Soil is actually very different depending on where you are, even from one garden to the next. Local conditions have a great influence on the kind of soil that forms. In areas with lots of sandstone, soils are usually nutrient-poor and don't hold water very well, whereas in areas with lots of limestone, soils are rich in nutrients. Different types of soil suit different types of plants; gardeners talk of lime-loving and lime-hating plants,

**Soil helps clean our water, protects against floods, and plays a crucial role in carbon cycling.**

for example, and the difference in plants you might see when walking from chalky meadow into a forest is partly due to the soil.

However, it would be a mistake to think of this as a one-way relationship. Plants depend on soil, but they themselves play a central role in making it. They do this by contributing organic matter to the soil when they die, as they break down through the process of decomposition. Plant roots also aid soil formation by breaking up rocks and helping to mix the mineral and organic components together, as well as holding the resulting soil in place when it is threatened by wind or water.

All this sounds simple and straightforward, but it's a long process: it takes around 400 years to create a layer of soil just half an inch thick. A further challenge is that many human actions can very quickly cause soil damage. Intensive agriculture can lead to a loss of nutrients, and one of the lesser-known consequences of rain forest clearance is the damage caused to soil, which is rapidly washed away by rain when tree roots are no longer there to hold it in place.

42

## Soil Profile

Soil is formed in distinct layers called horizons, each of which has its own characteristics. There are five main types and the sequence of horizons is known as a soil profile.

**Horizon O:** Also known as the organic layer, this surface layer is rich in nutrients as it is made up of dead plant material.

**Horizon A:** Known as topsoil, this layer is made up of organic matter and minerals. As it is very nutrient-rich, it's the layer where you find many plants and animals living.

**Horizon B:** The subsoil layer is made up mainly of clay. Although it has less organic matter than the layer above, it still contains lots of minerals, which have been washed down from the higher levels.

**Horizon C:** This layer is known as the parent material because it is made up mainly of large rocks from which the other layers are formed by erosion.

**Horizon R:** This layer, also known as bedrock, is a solid mass of rock that lies several feet beneath the surface.

## Soil Texture Classification

Scientists have created a way of characterizing the many different soil types based on their texture. A soil can be classified into one of twelve types depending on the proportion of sand, silt, or clay particles that it is made up of.

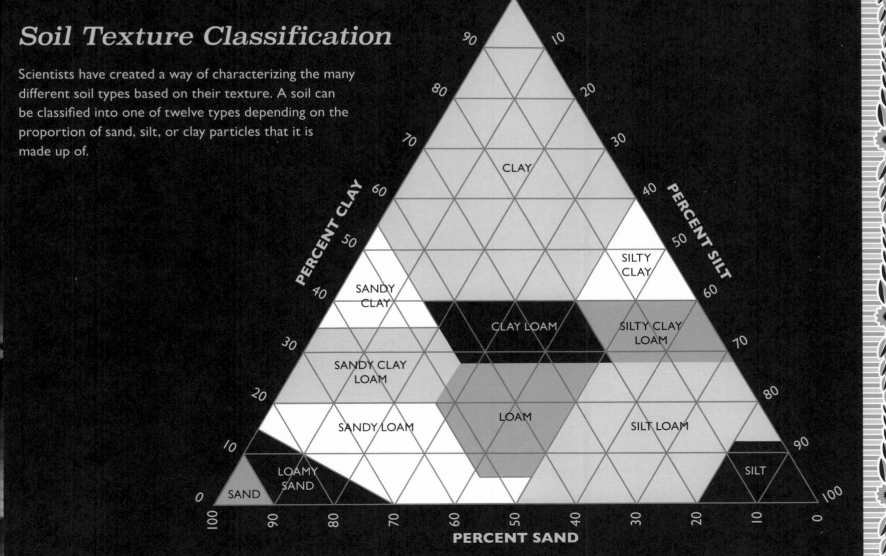

# PLANTS IN DESERTS

**Like all living things, plants need water to survive. Some, though, can get by on very little. The best known are those iconic desert plants, cacti.**

THE CACTUS FAMILY, or Cactaceae, comprises around 1,700 species, all but one of which are native to the Americas. A few of these species live in moist forests, but most are dryland plants that have evolved a range of adaptations for coping with a scarcity of water. Their stems are usually swollen and act as water stores, often having ribs or tubercles that can expand or contract depending on the amount of water inside. Their roots often spread out over wide areas to take maximum advantage of what little rainfall there is or penetrate deep underground to reach subterranean sources of water.

Most have dispensed with leaves. These are very useful for photosynthesizing but tend to go through a lot of precious water, through transpiration,

**The largest cacti can grow up to 66 feet/20 meters tall and weigh as much as a car.**

when doing so. Instead, photosynthesis takes place in cells on the outside of the stems, which have a waxy coating that cuts down on water loss. Many species also have a dense covering of spines or woolly fibers. In addition to helping protect the cactus from predators, these coverings create a zone of still air around the plants, which further helps reduce transpiration.

Perhaps the most cunning adaptation that cacti possess, however, is less immediately obvious. It's how they operate their stomata, the tiny openings that enable plants to absorb carbon dioxide for photosynthesis. The trouble is that when it is hot and sunny, as it often is during the day in deserts, open stomata lose a lot of water through transpiration. Cacti and a number of other arid-land plants have evolved a system whereby they keep their stomata shut during the day and open them at night, when there is little transpiration. Carbon dioxide enters and is converted into a chemical called malic acid, which the plant stores and uses the next day as the basis for photosynthesis, when there is plenty of sunshine to power the process.

# SIXTEEN KINDS OF CACTI

1. *Stenocactus* sp.
2. *Astrophytum asterias*
3. *Echinocactus grusonii*
4. *Ariocarpus retusus*
5. *Leuchtenbergia principis*
6. *Haageocereus decumbens*
7. Prickly pear (*Opuntia* sp.)
8. *Carnegiea gigantea*
9. *Lophophora williamsii*
10. *Schlumbergera* sp.
11. *Pereskiopsis spathula*
12. *Cleistocactus straussii*
13. *Echinopsis* sp.
14. *Tephrocactus geometricus*
15. Turk's cap (*Melocactus*)
16. *Mammillaria* sp.

# PLANTS IN WATER

**Curiously, just as too little water creates problems for plants, so does too much. That helps explain why relatively few plant species are adapted to life in it.**

**P**ERHAPS THE MOST important problem faced by water plants is the fact that the concentrations of both the carbon dioxide used in photosynthesis and the oxygen needed for respiration are typically much lower in water than in the atmosphere. While only the photosynthesizing parts of a plant need access to carbon dioxide, all living parts, including roots, generally need oxygen. Land plants rely on tiny air pockets in the soil to supply oxygen to their roots, but submerged and waterlogged soils usually have little or no oxygen in them at all.

Aquatic and wetland plants have come up with various ways of dealing with this. Many of them grow partially out of the water or float on the surface, where they are exposed to the air. They often contain a spongy tissue called aerenchyma, which is full of cavities and channels that can store gases and move them from one part of a plant to another. Those with above-water parts can use these

**Aquatic plants help filter water, removing carbon dioxide and keeping it clean for fish.**

channels to carry air directly to submerged parts, including roots and rhizomes. Plants that grow wholly underwater often use aerenchyma to help recycle gases: they store both the carbon dioxide created by respiring cells and the oxygen generated through photosynthesis. These plants may also make use of other forms of dissolved carbon, notably carbonate ions, in addition to dissolved carbon dioxide when they photosynthesize.

Even in clear water, the amount of sunlight available for photosynthesis decreases quite fast with increasing depth. Underwater plants usually have thin leaves rich in chloroplasts to take advantage of what light there is, but even so, they can usually grow successfully only in fairly shallow water.

# AQUATIC PLANTS

## Seagrass beds

Only about sixty kinds of flowering plants, collectively known as seagrasses, are adapted to life entirely in the ocean. They form extensive underwater meadows, an important habitat for animals.

## Mangroves

Mangroves are trees and shrubs that grow partially underwater along coasts and estuaries in the tropics and subtropics. They grow in oxygen-poor sediments and have rootlike structures above the soil that are equipped with breathing pores.

## Reeds

Soils in freshwater swamps are often rich in nutrients but contain little or no free oxygen. Phragmites reeds blow air through their stems into their roots.

## Lake Plants

Many freshwater plants have floating leaves connected to rhizomes by stems packed with aerenchyma, spongy tissue that provides buoyancy and serves as a reservoir and channel for gases.

# RAIN FORESTS

**Of all the world's many natural habitats, tropical rain forests are home to the largest number of different plant and animal species.**

**T**HE DIVERSITY of tropical rain forests is staggering. A 2½ acre/ 1 hectare area of rain forest in South America may have three times as many different kinds of trees growing in it as there are in the whole of Europe. And it's not just the trees that are diverse. These forests cover just 6 percent or so of the world's land area (and the amount is shrinking all the time) yet are believed to contain a good half of all the world's living species.

To an earthbound visitor, this immense variety may not be obvious at first sight. The trunks of many rain forest trees look very similar to one another, and the ground vegetation is often quite sparse—the canopy overhead casts such deep shade that only plants adapted to low levels of light can thrive beneath it. Close inspection, however, will reveal a surprising variety of plants—far more than would be found on the ground in a temperate woodland or coniferous forest.

**The Amazon rain forest provides 20 percent of the Earth's oxygen.**

Yet it's only when venturing into the forest canopy, high off the ground, that the real extent of the diversity becomes apparent. Here the range of leaf shapes and growth forms makes it clear just how many different kinds of trees are growing. Moreover, and in sharp contrast to temperate and cold-climate forests, a vast range of orchids, ferns, and other plants make their home here as epiphytes, clinging with their roots to the branches and trunks of trees. These canopy plants in turn provide homes for animals of all kinds.

From the forest floor to the tops of the tallest trees, the amount of sunlight, water, and wind that the organisms living in rain forests are exposed to varies. This diversity of environmental conditions means that very different plants are able to grow in each layer of the forest.

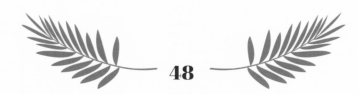

48

# LAYERS OF A TROPICAL RAIN FOREST

**EMERGENT LAYER**
The emergent layer is the highest level of the rain forest. Here, the tall trees have to cope with extreme environmental conditions: hot sun, drenching rain, and steady winds. Trees in this layer often have very waxy leaves, which protect them from the sun.

**CANOPY**
The canopy is the densest and probably the most diverse layer of the rain forest.

Here, leaves and branches are closely packed together, limiting the amount of water and light that reaches the layers below.

**UNDERSTORY**
Only a small amount of light reaches the understory, so the plants that grow here are mostly smaller and are adapted to shady conditions.

FOREST FLOOR Very little light (approximately 2 percent) manages to reach the forest floor, so only plants adapted to low sunlight, such as moss, can grow here. This layer provides perfect conditions for fungi.

EMERGENT LAYER

CANOPY

UNDERSTORY

FLOOR LAYER

# PLANT HOT SPOTS

**Like tropical rain forests, shrublands in areas with a Mediterranean climate also support huge numbers of different plant species, many of them confined to small areas.**

ANYONE WITH EVEN a passing interest in plants who took a walk in a nature reserve in the Western Cape of South Africa in late winter or early spring would quickly realize they were somewhere special. They would be surrounded by a bewildering variety of plants in flower, with new kinds appearing at every turn.

Like the Mediterranean Basin, coastal California, central Chile, and southwest Australia, the Western Cape is a plant biodiversity hot spot, with a richness in plant species rivaling that of the most diverse tropical rain forest. These areas all share a similar climate, with cool, rainy winters and warm or hot dry summers. The main type of vegetation in each is also similar, in appearance at least, being dominated by shrubs, often spiky and with small, tough leaves. There are relatively few small trees and many different kinds of geophytes, plants that grow from underground bulbs, corms, or tubers.

**Mediterranean ecosystems are some of the most endangered regions on Earth.**

All these areas are extraordinarily rich in plant species but curiously, and quite unlike rain forests, do not have an unusually large range of animals living in them. The richest and most distinctive of all is the Western Cape, where more than 9,000 different plant species, two-thirds of which are found nowhere else, grow in an area less than half the size of the United Kingdom (which has a mere 1,600 or so native plant species).

There are a number of different theories as to why these areas are as rich in plants as they are. It may have to do with how long they have had a stable climate, or it might be related to the frequency of fires, which are generally common, or with the way many of the plants are pollinated (often by flies) or their seeds dispersed (often by ants). None of these, though, quite adds up to a convincing whole, and the puzzle of these areas' high diversity remains one of the most intriguing in biology.

# TEN PLANTS THAT FEED THE WORLD

We humans rely directly or indirectly on plants for a whole range of necessities: clothing, building materials, fuel, the oxygen we breathe, and, of course, food—the vast majority of which we get from farming.

## Corn

Around 1 billion metric tons/1.1 billion tons of corn are produce each year. Corn is now the world's biggest grain crop, although half the crop is used for animal feed. This is a wasteful way of fe people: it takes around 13 pounds/6 kilograms of corn to produ pounds/1 kilogram of beef, for example. Much of the rest is pro into corn syrup, oil, and starch.

## RICE

Around 830,000 tons/ 750 million metric tons of rice are produced each year. Over half the world's population relies on it as a staple, with more than 500 million people getting more than half their energy intake from it. Unlike most other bulk crops, much of the world's rice is grown on small farms.

## Tomatoes

About 200,000 tons/180,000 metric tons of tomatoes are produced in a year.

A high proportion of the world's soybean crop (360,000 tons/330,000 metric tons a year) is turned into animal feed.

## Soybeans

## Sugarcane

Sugarcane is the world's biggest crop by weight (nearly 2.2 billion tons/2 billion metric tons a year) because the whole plant, not just the seed, is harvested. A large portion of the crop is used to produce fuel.

## POTATOES

420,000 tons/ 380,000 metric tons produced a year

Of the many tens of thousands of edible plant species, only a tiny proportion are cultivated and an even smaller number—just ten or so—provide the great bulk of the world's food. Of these, three kinds of grass—corn, wheat, and rice—are of paramount importance. Their seeds, known as grain, provide more than half the energy needs of the world's human population as well as a high proportion of its protein needs—either directly or indirectly, through meat from animals that are fed on grain.

## Cassava

Cassava (310,000 tons/ 280,000 metric tons a year) is a hugely important crop in developing nations, especially in Africa, where many people rely on it for their survival.

## Bananas and Plantains

165,000 tons/150,000 metric tons produced a year

beans

Soybeans

## Palm Oil

Palm oil production (330,000 tons/300,000 metric tons a year) has increased steeply in the past few decades. Vast areas of rain forest have been cleared to grow this lucrative crop.

## WHEAT

Around 830,000 tons/750 million metric tons of wheat are produced each year. It is the world's most extensive crop, grown on over 770,000 square miles/two million square kilometers of land, most of it in vast, uniform fields.

# GROWING FOR THE FUTURE

**Producing enough food to sustain the world's seven billion people is an amazing achievement, but it comes at a cost. Modern industrial farming methods often cause immense environmental damage. Is there a better way of doing things?**

LARGE-SCALE FARMING requires the input of huge amounts of energy and of chemical fertilizers, insecticides, fungicides, and herbicides. It can lead to pollution, erosion, the breakdown of soils, and the exhaustion of precious water resources. It has also caused massive losses of biodiversity, as rich and varied natural habitats have been converted into landscapes dominated by a few crops. Moreover, plants grown on a large scale are themselves vulnerable to the spread of disease and to rapid environmental shifts that are likely to become more extreme and common as the world's climate heats up.

**One sustainable approach to farming and gardening is called permaculture.**

To address these issues, people everywhere are turning to more sustainable and resilient ways of producing food, both by experimenting with new methods and by applying approaches that have been in use for thousands of years. Sustainable farming usually takes its inspiration from natural systems. Instead of vast fields devoted to one crop, for instance, a range of different plants may be grown together, encouraging natural pest control agents and pollinators. Organic waste is recycled, and the use of synthetic chemicals is reduced or eliminated altogether. Water is applied sparingly and soil disturbance kept to a minimum so that underground organisms can do their work in supporting plant growth.

Low-input small-scale farming that uses many of these methods already plays a vital role in feeding rural people in developing countries. However, these approaches currently provide only a small proportion of the food consumed in the developed world, where it's difficult for producers to compete commercially with intensive farming.

# A PERMACULTURE GARDEN

This is what a sustainable permaculture garden might look like. It's a sort of self-sufficient ecosystem.

# SACRED AND SYMBOLIC PLANTS

### Just a few kinds of plants provide most of humanity's basic nutritional needs, but far more are used and valued in other ways.

**T**ENS OF THOUSANDS of different plants and plant parts are used worldwide for a variety of purposes, including as medicinal herbs and stimulants; as spices, flavorings, and perfumes; and as ornamentals to beautify people's surroundings, as well as for more prosaic purposes such as building materials, clothing, and fuel.

Some plants also take on cultural or religious significance. This may happen because a plant plays a central role in the livelihood of a particular group of people. The date palm, for example, was historically crucial for the survival of desert-dwelling people in

**Many religions have their own sacred plant.**

the Middle East. It is not surprising, then, that it is of symbolic importance in both Judaism and Christianity, religions whose origins lie in that part of the world. Similarly, the kapok tree was much used by the Mayan people of Mesoamerica and Central America, and it too became an important cultural emblem, appearing on pottery and other artworks.

A plant need not be of practical use to become an important symbol, however. The lotus is a central symbol in Buddhism and was also revered in ancient Egypt because of the way its beautiful flowers emerge from muddy and unclean waters.

Many sacred plants are associated with healing and well-being. A high proportion of these do indeed contain active ingredients that can help us. Often these have effects related to traditional uses. Willow, for example, one of the "Four Species" ritually used during the Jewish celebration of Sukkot and long known for its ability to relieve pain, is the origin of aspirin. Sometimes, though, plants turn out to have very unexpected properties: in the 1960s, it was discovered that extracts from the bark of the yew, a tree associated with ancient sacred sites in Europe, contains a powerful anticancer agent that has proved invaluable in treating many forms of the disease.

# SACRED PLANTS

1. *Sacred fig*: native to tropical Asia; sacred in Buddhism
2. *Boswellia*: produces a resin known as frankincense, featured in the Christian Nativity story
3. *Mistletoe*: used in ancient Celtic rituals to cure infertility
4. *Commiphora*: produces myrrh resin, also featured in the Nativity story
5. *Nardostachys jatamansi*: the source of spikenard, an oil used medicinally

6. *Sacred bamboo*: used to decorate temples at the Lunar New Year
7. *Basil*: native to Asia; sacred in Hinduism
8. *Yew*: long-living; revered as holy and eternal
9. *Lotus*: symbolizes purity in Buddhism and Hinduism
10. *Bay*: used to represent wisdom and success in ancient Greece
11. *Kapok*: connects the three levels of earth in Mayan mythology
12. *The Four Species:* used in the Jewish celebration of Sukkot:
a. *Willow,* b. *Date palm,* c. *Myrtle,* d. *Fruit of the citron tree*

# COLLECTING PLANTS

Gardeners are often passionate about the plants they grow and may wish to collect particular groups of plants from around the world. Thi[s] can develop into rivalry, with collectors vying to assemble the most impressive collections. Competitive plant collecting was a particularly [...] pastime in nineteenth-century Britain, often involving the importation of new plants from areas colonized into the British Empire.

TROPICAL PLANTS

1. *Aeschynanthus lobbianus*
2. *Hoya fraterna*
3. *Medinilla magnifica*
4. *Thunbergia lutea*
5. *Fuchsia dependens*
6. *Lapageria rosea*
7. *Anthurium veitchii*
8. *Sonerila margaritacea*
9. *Nepenthes rajah*
10. *Nepenthes burkei*
11. *Ixora lobbii*
12. *Dieffenbachia bowmannii*

esses sprang up to meet this demand. The largest and most celebrated was that of the Veitch family, who employed a network of
tors to acquire plants from all over the world for their nurseries. The Veitches specialized in tender species that needed to be grown in
houses or conservatories in Britain, tropical orchids being a particular fad at the time. Over the decades, they introduced hundreds of
lants into cultivation in the UK. Some are rarely grown now, but others have become familiar house or garden plants.

ORCHIDS

13. *Dendrobium farmeri*
14. *Pleione humilis*
15. *Vanda coerulea*
16. *Phragmipedium caudatum*
17. *Sobralia dichotoma*
18. *Paphiopedilum lowii*
19. *Ascocentrum miniatum*
20. *Calanthe rosea*
21. *Bulbophyllum lobbii*
22. *Vanda tricolor*
23. *Dendrobium albosanguineum*
24. *Paphiopedilum niveum*

Veitch & Sons

# BREEDING PLANTS

**Introducing species from the wild is one way of increasing the range of plants that can be grown. Creating new varieties from those already in cultivation is another. Tulips are a prime example of this.**

THE FIRST RECORDS of tulips in cultivation come from thirteenth-century Turkey, but they were almost certainly grown long before this in gardens in central Asia, where numerous wild species are found. From there they made their way west to Turkey and then in the sixteenth century to Europe, where they caused a sensation, first in France and then in the Netherlands. There, plant breeders set to work trying to create new varieties. It was slow and laborious work sowing seeds collected from bulbs that had flowered that year, growing the seedlings until they flowered—which could take up to eight years—selecting the most desirable ones and reproducing them from side-shoots.

Since growers lacked an understanding of genetics, their work proceeded by trial and error. This was made even more complicated by the fact that the most desirable forms, so-called

**In the 1630s, certain tulips were so valuable that they cost more than a house.**

Rembrandt tulips, whose flowers had beautiful streaks of different colors, were the product of viral infections and could not be produced by breeding. They occurred rarely, and it was difficult to keep particular types going since the virus weakened the stock over the years. Their scarcity led wealthy collectors to pay higher and higher prices as part of a highly speculative and risky tulip "futures" market. Fortunes were made—and then lost when the boom crashed and prices collapsed in February 1637.

Tulip breeding is still slow work: it takes about twenty years from the initial crossbreeding to building up a large enough stock of the desirable offspring to release them for sale. This has not deterred plant breeders, though. There are currently more than 6,500 named tulip varieties, and the number increases every year. Almost all are derived from just three or four wild species first grown in Persian gardens centuries ago.

# THE SIXTEEN GROUPS OF TULIPS

1. Single Early – Couleur Cardinal
2. Double Early – Peach Blossom
3. Triumph – Shirley
4. Darwin Hybrid – Ad Rem
5. Single Late – Queen of the Night
6. Lily-Flowered – Ballade
7. Fringed – Red Hat
8. Viridiflora – Spring Green
9. Rembrandt – Zomerschoon
10. Parrot – Black Parrot
11. Double Late – Orange Princess
12. Kaufmanniana – Showwinner
13. Fosteriana – Purissima
14. Greigii – Red Riding Hood
15. Miscellaneous – Tulipa clusiana
16. Coronet – Elegant Crown

# PLANTS IN PERIL

## Florida
### *ASIMINA TETRAMERA*

There are approximately 950 plants of this fire-adapted species, which is under threat because of fire suppression by humans.

## Iberian Peninsula
### *IRIS BOISSIERI*

There are fewer than 11,000 plants of this species. Its main threats are plant collectors and habitat loss from forest plantations.

## England
### *THAMNOBRYUM ANGUSTIFOLIUM*

This moss species is found only on c[...] in Derbyshire and is under threat fr[...] collectors and changes in water l[...]

## California
### *LILIUM OCCIDENTALE*

This species is under threat from livestock grazing and trampling.

## Mexico
### *MAMMILLARIA HERRERAE*

This species is found in just one location. Poaching has led to a 95 percent population decline in 20 years.

NORTH AMERICA

ATLANTIC OCEAN

E[...]

Equator

PACIFIC OCEAN

SOUTH AMERICA

Rain forests

## Tropical South America
### *ANIBA ROSAEODORA*

This tree has been unsustainably harvested for its essential oil.

## Andes
### *PUYA RAIMONDII*

The main threats to this plant come from fires caused by humans, as well as habitat loss.

## Chile/Argentina
### *FITZROYA CUPRESSO[...]*

This tree has been both exploite[...] cleared to make room for agricultur[...] take 100 years for a tree to reach m[...]

five plant species is at risk of extinction. Species with small distributions are especially vulnerable, and although some small distributions
naturally, many are the result of human activity. Habitat destruction and exploitation are two of the largest threats to plants globally.

## Greece
### PAEONIA PARNASSICA

are fewer than 2,500 individuals of
autiful plant, which is under threat
due to plant collectors.

## Deserts of Northern China
### CISTANCHE DESERTICOLA

This parasitic plant is threatened by
exploitation of its host tree and by collection
for use in herbal medicine.

## Philippines
### NEPENTHES ATTENBOROUGHII

This rare and valuable species is
under threat from poachers. Fewer than 500
plants remain.

## Western Australia
### ACACIA AURATIFLORA

There are approximately 1,200 plants of
this species, its main threat being habitat
destruction.

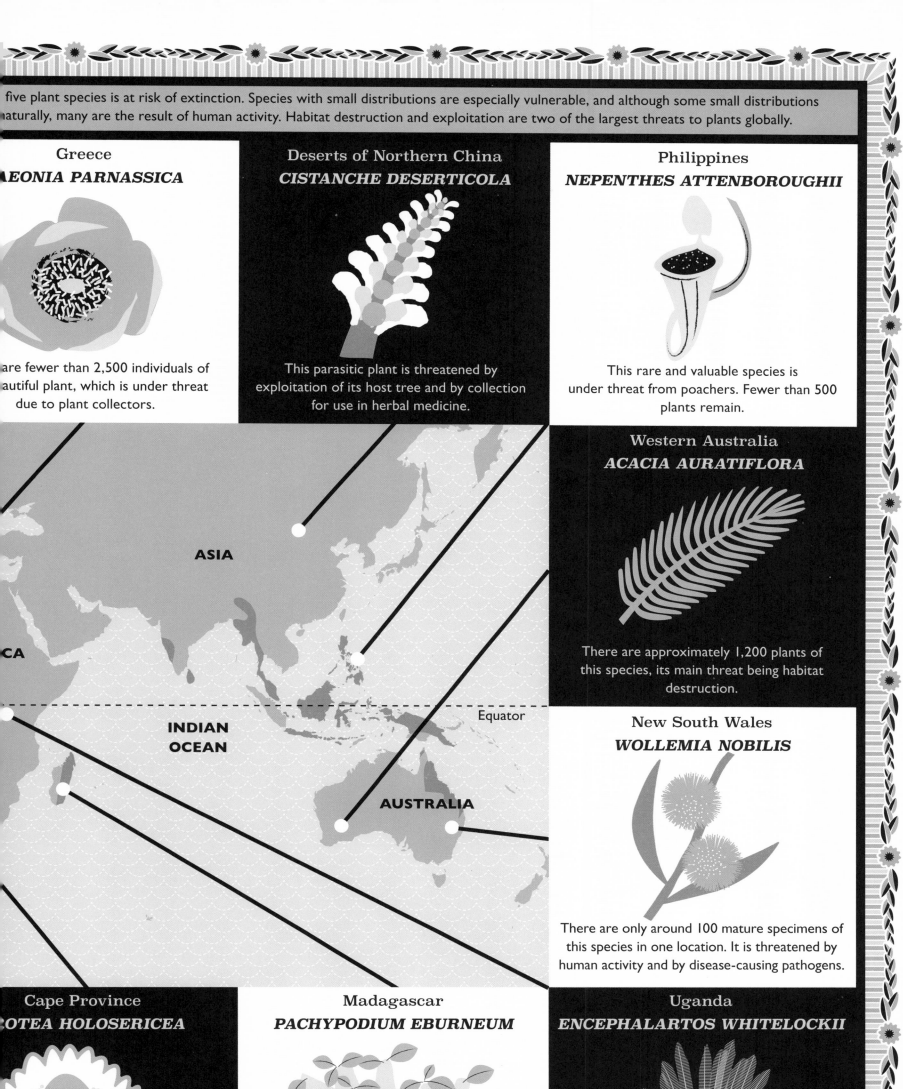

ASIA

INDIAN
OCEAN

Equator

AUSTRALIA

## New South Wales
### WOLLEMIA NOBILIS

There are only around 100 mature specimens of
this species in one location. It is threatened by
human activity and by disease-causing pathogens.

## Cape Province
### PROTEA HOLOSERICEA

pecies has been overharvested; its
g population extends to less than
are miles/15 square kilometers.

## Madagascar
### PACHYPODIUM EBURNEUM

There are fewer than 100 plants of this
species; it is under threat from plant
collectors and annual wildfires.

## Uganda
### ENCEPHALARTOS WHITELOCKII

There are approximately 8,000 mature plants
of this cycad, in just one location. The building
of a hydroelectric plant has led to habitat loss.

*For Nic and Rosie*
MJ

*In memory of my dad, Ken Brown*
JB

With thanks to Alison Eyres for reviewing the text

First US edition 2021
First published by Walker Studio, an imprint of Walker Books (UK), 2019

Library of Congress Catalog Card Number pending
ISBN 978-1-5362-1532-8

20 21 22 23 24 25 LEO 10 9 8 7 6 5 4 3 2 1

Printed in Heshan, Guangdong, China

This book was typeset in Gill Sans and Superclarendon.
The illustrations were created digitally.

Candlewick Studio
an imprint of
Candlewick Press
99 Dover Street
Somerville, Massachusetts 02144

www.candlewickstudio.com